A Flight Odyssey

A COLLECTION OF POEMS BY
DOLLIE CARPENTER YOUKELES

Introduction by
JAY PAUL

*For Angela and Don
special best wishes
Dollie C. Youkeles*

ROAD
PUBLISHERS

"Books Worth Your Time"
33412 Lankford Hwy. • Painter, VA 23420

Published by **ROAD Publishers**
33412 Lankford Highway
Painter, Virginia 23420-0431

Printed in the United States of America

Photographs by Lila B. Youkeles

Book & Cover Design by Donna L. Robinson

Library of Congress Catalog No. 94-67992

ISBN 1-880016-16-8

ACKNOWLEDGMENTS

The author and publisher express grateful acknowledgment to the following
publications in which some of these poems first appeared: *Pleasant Living*
("Red-Tailed Hawk," "Tracking Birds in Snow") *The Progress-Index*
("Last Flight").

Dedicated

to Abe, who won his wings in World War II
with B-24s in Italy. I wonder,
still, how those brave young men ever knew
the will it took to test the wild blue yonder.

Table of Contents

Introduction

*I was in another mind, which I liked better
than the one I had. The birds were in it; and
what they would do, I would try to follow
and pick up, and go on.*
James Dickey, *To the White Sea*

In 1988 a gruff, quick-to-laugh woman with wavy, grey-white hair appeared at a workshop on the Christopher Newport University campus, declaring her intention after years of silence to write poems. But undeclared: she was mourning her husband—dead several years. She was seeking not only voice, but, to judge from poems she's written since, transformation. And like James Dickey's character, she would make flying things her image and guide.

Spunky, tough, daring—that's sexagenarian Dollie Youkeles of "Paper Kites"; wishing she were "game enough on judgment day" to "give a fiver just to send my soul / up to heaven spread-eagled on a kite." Likewise, four decades before, aboard the troopship *Matsonia* in the Pacific, fretting about enemy subs and sweat that wouldn't wash away, she trusted in "legions" of flying fish that "swam shotgun for us."

After working in journalism and public relations and raising a son and daughter, Youkeles lives, enviably, beside the Ware River in tidewater Virginia. Like any poet or scientist or curious human being, she ponders mysteries, like "how far out to sea" gulls may trail ships and "what despair / of sea made them go / with Brigham Young to share / his Utah haven." Gifts, such as whistling swans "half suspended through the ice" and a pair of rare bald eagles quarreling over food for an hour, lighten—if not redeem—this poet's mortality. And who can resist her red-eyed vireo: "That rufous-rumped, buff-bellied stalker / dares to raise binoculars at me!"

As funny as Youkeles can be, faith can never be far from her thoughts. A sandpiper feeding "one beat beyond / a crashing tidal grave." A dove recovered from a hunter's shot—"He flew one day, more surprised than we." And more directly:

Sail planers, alone among birdmen,

find silence between the cloud and sod
to listen for the voice of God.

I like to think of the many presences she embodies—this woman who studied with Theodore Roethke and William Carlos Williams, who loves Bach and Billie Holiday, who's collected air-mail stamps for sixty years, who heard Dylan Thomas and Edith Sitwell perform. One hears, perhaps, Dame Edith's brittle music in these lines on the loon: "dreary in winter drab, / maniacal laugh / kee-a-ree ringing."

As you read Youkeles' poems, you'll see they're more than pretty. She's feisty, vigorous. After all, she praises the Laughing Gull above other varieties, exulting that it "soars / above them all on a thermal," sailing "around around around." When playing-in-language and informed observation become one— as in "Red-Breasted Merganser Ducks" and "The Leaf That Moved" and more—Dollie Youkeles's delight enters the reader's head.

Jay Paul
Newport News, Virginia

Jay Paul chairs the English department at Christopher Newport University and also directs the Honors Program. His teaching interests include American literature, but emphasize creative writing. He participated in the first two Chesapeake Poetry Festivals and frequently gives readings and conducts workshops. Among his greatest satisfactions have been a collaboration with painter Jon Petruchyk and working with gifted writers, some of whose work has won national awards and recognition.

Nearly 200 of Jay Paul's poems have appeared in magazines around the United States—*Poetry Northwest, The Christian Century, Southwest Review, Mississippi Valley Review, New Virginia Review,* and *Southern Poetry Review,* to name several. Recent work appears in *Shenandoah, Artemis,* and *Mockingbird.* His fiction has appeared in *The Crescent Review* and *New England Review.* A story, "Aunt Titus Nusbaum Toots in from Titusville," published in *Cimarron Review,* received Honorable Mention in Houghton Mifflin's *Best American Short Stories.*

A native of upstate New York, he lived in the midwest before moving to Newport News, Virginia, where he shares a house and garden with his wife, Joanne, and occasionally their daughter, Catherine, a doctoral student at the University of Michigan.

I.

Wonder

"There be three things which are too wonderful for me, yea, four which I know not: The way of an eagle in the air; the way of a serpent upon a rock; the way of a ship in the midst of the sea; and the way of a man with a maid."

—Proverbs: XXX, 18

To Fly

I sing of wings and things that fly,
cherish the loft of rising wind,
sound of wings that I must envy,
mundanely rooted to the ground.

There's consolation in my song!
These slender lyrics loosed are free
to touch the hearts of listeners,
the poet's fancy taking flight.

Ostrich

The shameless she-male ostrich
    asserts herself in final test
as matriarchal bossterich.

While she's out disporting with the band,
    the he-male guards the family nest
and hides his head beneath the sand.

Mourning Dove

If ever a dove was in mourning,
this one was. The children
brought it home, beseeching me
"to fix it."
—as if love alone could mend
the bone-raw broken wing!
    (Dove season was only one day old
    and there would be others;
    fallen in the fields, buckshot-
    bruised and dirt-smeared
    where blood oozed red on grey.)
We kept him through the winter in a cage
of laundry baskets. The task-at-hand
was to make him eat and
to make him understand that
hands are gentle, too.

At first he sat a sullen, huddled heap
of feathers, and turned an arrogant tail
to our entreaties. The beak,
a curved rapacious thing, was quick
to seek offending hands.
The millet (French-imported)
turned the trick. He repaired,
resenting all the while captivity.

In the spring we had the first
of several launchings.
Each time the weakened wing
flew erratically around
half circles, ending on the ground.

    (But God must keep his eye
    alike on doves and sparrows
    against the slings and arrows
    of outrageous hunters.)

He flew one day, more surprised than we,
to the nearest tree
and sat there blinking.
Then he tried a farther limb
and the forest reclaimed him—
free,
never looking back.
We wished him well.

Blue Jay

A caucus of raucous jays—
king-crested and cocky,
resplendent in suits of light,
bright as blue velvet—
in all their jay-walking days
they never bit a boy
or stole his eggs.

Dead
they bring no honor
to the hunter. The truth is
there are no bad jays,
only bad boys with
slingshots.

Red-Winged Blackbird

I saw ten blackbirds on a hill
glistening black against the light—
quarreling, cravening, cawing, shrill—
iridescent, fluttering fright.

Then a flash of crimson wing,
blood-bright as from the hunter's gun;
I saw ten blackbirds taking flight
—and then there were none.

The Red-Tailed Hawk

struck so swiftly I could scarcely see
the rush of wings and terror of the talons
that impaled the squirrel on the tree. A gasp,
mine, proclaimed the death of one small rodent

that dropped into the grass. My window-watch
had spied this haughty fellow high in a pine,
perched and posing, looking for such a meal.
I guess I wasn't ready for the kill.

He took his time to flutter to the ground,
a show of speckled wings and rust-red tail.
There was no *coup de grâce;* he knew his grand
talent had never failed to kill his prey.

I mourned the squirrel, marveled at the shock,
muttered to myself that nature's balance
was often cruel to human eyes. Indeed—
no need at all to humanize a hawk.

Luna Moth

Moon moth, pale green
as moon cheese seen
darkly through clouds;
night-goddess Selene.

Risk moon-madness between
four painted ocelli
and lunar green beam
unseeing and seen.

Can four eyes mean
that swallow-tail moths
see equally keen on nights
devoid of moon's beam?

Six Insect-O-Grams

Monarchs
  reign

over royal
kingdoms
in the air

Frenzied

is
the mayfly's
dance to death
for
  life

Praise the
  praying
  mantis

who goes
a-preying
  as a
walking stick
and prays
for his victim

Firefly
  pyrotechnicrats

illuminate
inseminate
  and
duplicate

Dragonfly

is
pond perfect
practitioner
  of
    aerial ballet

Moth

loves light
and flame
  more than life

II.

World

"O world, I cannot hold thee close enough."
—Edna St. Vincent Millay,
"God's World"

No Place to Hide

The eagle and the mole, she said,
    shun the spotted sight and sound
soaring safely overhead
    and burrowing beneath the ground.

Dear Elinor Wylie;
since your death in '28
    we've come an atomic moon around,
fouling the cliff inviolate
    and places velvet moles are found.

Riposte

The mynah bird
awoke at dawn for another
day of humanizing,

assumed the preferred
perch position near the
little mirror that

reflected dim memories of
trees and flight,

preened, for one-half hour,
the aerodynamically-engineered
feathers of his wings,

watched with head properly cocked
as his human cleaned the
golden cage of bars,

said "good morning" and
dutifully accepted the piece of apple,

recognized the refilled dish of
seed and bowl of water
for what they were

and compulsively interrupted
the blathering comments of
his human.

The mynah bird proclaimed
to all his world:
"Flight and time and sky and heaven
are only tested by the will."

No one had taught him such things.
They said he didn't have the skill.

Starling Stories

Starlings skewered "en broche"
along the humming wires
broadcast spring's approach,
herald autumn's fires.

Nothing to Crow About

Five big, black crows that first white day
and that was all, splayed feet sinking
in the snow. They sailed and sallied
from limb to ground, wheeling around,

more cat-conscious than the smallest
tufted-titmouse who stood its ground
and claimed the corn. The crows cawed dark,
dire threats, bleakest shadings of sound.

Blackest of nightmares, holocaust
of fear, a hundred crows returned
and took the corn. The titmouse won,
however, bills down, one on one.

Sandpiper

Agile sandpiper, racing
with each receding wave,
tracing tidal patterns
on slender, daring feet;
black bill thrusting
for the sustenance
the sea offers in retreat
just one beat beyond
a crashing tidal grave.

Cardinal

The saintly, crested cardinal wears
bright red raiment and bears
no malice to other birds.
His glory is too great for words.
We know him without indecision
streaking-red across our vision.

Feeding Station in Winter

A winged crowd attends my winter feast
of suet pudding, cracked scratch corn and seed.
Winter's need, of course, had brought them flocking.
I stand no nearer to them now than ever,
a wary, human window-watcher. Yet
let me think that winter snow has bound
us, the birds and me, in unspoken pact.

My winter feast nourishes their living,
while their presence nourishes my loving.

#5 Seagull

#1

    seagull, a Herring Gull,
    calls a mate, struts
    along the dock

#2

    seagull, a Glaucous Gull, dives for fish,
    squawks revenge
    for trespassers

#3

    seagull, a Kittiwake, balanced
    on one foot, sleeps,
    facing into wind

#4

    seagull, a Fulmar, preens
    a wing, a leg,
    a breast

#5

    seagull, a Laughing Gull, soars
    above them all, on a thermal
    that sails him
        around around around

Winter Notes From a Ware River Journal

I

A Red Letter Day the Ware river wears a new sheath of shining ice with just a narrow open current of water moving in the middle and there at the edge of this stream two bald eagles are eating a fish a bird watcher's dream I suck icecold air into my lungs in a surprised gasp a recent news story reported an Audubon birders' count of only four bald eagles residing in our county here are two of them so close these are adults with dark bodies and white heads and tails a quarrelling couple fighting over the food and eating at a distance from each other I watched enthralled for an hour breathing in bone chilling air and breathing out pride and majesty that emanated in eagle waves I think they dipped their wings to me as they flew off into the trees

II

My Chinese flying fish kite windsock a gorgeous golden
carp has broken its moorings in a winter storm flown away
from its tall pole on my dock carp belong in water but not
this silken beauty whose proper element was the air it joined
the Santa Claus wind sock and the one with the American
flag design flying away to a watery grave they added to a
growing list of flotsam and jetsam lost from my dock one fish
pole pulled away by a giant ray an aluminum chair a pocket
knife and two crab pots that didn't stay anchored I feel
appropriately guilty for adding this pollution to the bottom
of the Ware River and the Chesapeake Bay but I don't miss
them except for the beautiful Chinese flying fish kite
windsock

III

The 96 whistling swans were a little late this year maybe
the cold weather and the thin coating of ice on the water
brought them here now their arrival always unites our
human community we flock to the waters edge to count
swans and take photos our whistlers are garrulous today
croaking at each other with unwhistlelike sound they seem to
be half suspended through the ice with legs in the water
floating together with their long necks held straight up they
look like a flotilla of white submarines with their periscopes
in up position then for feeding they turn completely upside
down with their tails in the air I presume their long necks
and beaks scour the bottom for food our Christmas present
was late this year but worth the wait

IV

    While watching swans with my neighbor my little dog
Bandit undertook some frantic and spirited bird searching on
his own scurrying through the weeds on the river bank
produced a bird that Bandit carried off victoriously in his
mouth on the run I pursued him through three back yards
and onto his own home driveway where he deposited an
unhurt baby duck like bird it was not injured but was
strangely unfleet of foot on land propelling itself forward on
its breast pushing with its webbed feet I picked it up to check
for broken wings or tooth marks none it weighed about a
pound and had a white cheek I recalled the Audubon guide
description of the loon with its ungainly walk on land due to
the positioning of its feet far back on the body this was surely
a baby loon my neighbor agreed with me on the
identification and with Bandit incarcerated in the house I
released the baby loon on the shore Bandit has a soft mouth
my neighbor pronounced he'd make a good bird dog late
winter always surprises us with the miracles of spring

Seven Garden Insects in Haiku

HORSEFLY
Horsefly stings with fire.
Soars to escape flicking tail,
lands to bite again.

GNAT
Gnat buzzes close to ear.
Box your own head; gnat persists
risking sudden death.

MOSQUITO
Fragile blood-suckers;
mosquito bands fly by night,
disperse with the dawn.

WHITE MOTH
Furred, white antennas
do not warn of light and fire.
White moth, night's victim.

BEE
Ripe pear drips sugar
prized by harvest-tipsy bees,
food fit for a queen.

HORNET
Many summer boys,
knowing sweet barefoot delight,
feel hornet-quick wrath.

WASP
Adept architect,
builder of paper-thin houses,
fierce foe in defense.

III.

Wisdom

"Be ye therefore wise as serpents and
harmless as doves."
—New Testament, Matthew, X, 16

The Loon

Today one common loon,
feet first skidding,
landed on our river;
a loner, the first of many,
dreary in winter drab,
maniacal laugh
kee-a-ree ringing.

With miracle of spring
he turns painted porcelain
black and white art deco,
one not-so-common
and
one not-so-crazy
loon.

Rooster

Cock-sure of his hens,
the barnyard's afoul with him.
All crowing aside,
the rooster's the best booster we have
for the chicken population.
A businessman does well to emulate him:
Rise early,
tell the world about yourself,
preen your feathers for the girls,
and control your flock.
The hard part?
Convincing the competition
that you're not ready
to become
Coq au Vin.

Dodo

Poor dear dead dodo,
Didus ineptus—extinct
these many years.
Clumsy, flightless,
ceding Mauritius
to greedy man, fightless.

Civilization,
with power of the atom,
threatens disintegration,
offers no explanation.
Who is the dodo today;
who the bird of prey?

A Gathering of Gulls

for Stuart and his resident sea gulls

My neighbor's dock is galled with gulls
who gang there boldly while he mulls
revenge against bird-brained numbskulls.

His dock was more than sat upon.
His dock, in truth, was shat upon
and nearly painted white. "Begone,"

cried Stuart, hoisting up a fist
to chase away the galling tryst
of gulls, unloved upon his list

of birds. "Ah ha," he thought, "I've seen
the proper antidote. It's keen,
a great horned owl, one fierce of mien;

in plastic, sure, but they won't know.
It's said all birds fear owls, and so
my galling gang of gulls will go!"

It worked—two days—but then the howl
was ours (all he could cry was "Foul")
to see a gull perched on his owl.

Observations of a Red-Eyed Vireo

That rufous-rumped, buff-bellied stalker
    dares to raise binoculars at me!
He is, at best, a gravel-throated talker
    while I make magic music in a tree.

Not one of his fine-feathered flock can sing.
    I've heard them imitate our song. I think
they may be dead dodos resurrecting
    unsuccessful, lost life forms, on the brink.

Look at that ungainly pot-bellied shape!
    Aerodynamic form is for the birds
and wings that fail to fly are surely fake.
    Their species is too decadent for words.

Birds of a feather, I know, will flock together.
    We bird-brained watchers must protect our space,
take careful count of them in any weather
    and, just in general, keep them in their place.

Housefly

There came a day when scientists decided
    "If you can't beat 'em,
        join 'em."
—and right away, revelation:
    houseflies were not so bad after all!
        Insecticides were turned
to more peaceful uses,
    and abuses on fragile, flying bodies
        stopped.
Study topped study evaluating
    the not-so-common housefly;
        the advantage of six legs
and the ability to use them
    uncommonly well;
        the practicality of side-mounted eyes
for peripheral vision;
    the decision, by engineers, that wing span
        proportion to body was
aerodynamically perfect;
    discovery of a digestive tract
        that could tackle almost anything.
It seemed, in fact, too good to be true.
    The first mutation had wings
        the size of egg-beaters
and fell ingloriously back to earth.
    The next had need of work on feet
        that failed to grip the ceiling.
Another lacked the supersonic buzz.
    It was a time to try and fail
        and try again.
The noble work went on,
    whole generations in mutation
        —and soon
the first, perfect astronaut
    man-housefly winged off
        in victory to the moon.

Night Fliers

I know flying squirrels don't fly.
They say you really glide downward,
using flaps of skin to keep
you airborne. Nocturnal glider ace,
I prize your elevated place.

I've stood on the brink of banks and thought
it could work, if I believed enough.
Then I spread my wings and said
"I can fly" and willed myself
to test the emptiness of sky.

Well, I'm here now, flying squirrel,
watching you, still savoring flight.
We both can fly, my friend, or try.
At least you glide; myself, I find
I fly more safely in my mind.

IV.

Faith

"The reason birds can fly and we can't is simply that they have perfect faith, for to have faith is to have wings."

— James M. Barrie,
"The Little White Bird."

Baptism

I shared warm spring rain with birds in a wood.
The dampness I disliked, they thought good,
swelling a treetop chorus that startled me.
Silly birds, I thought, but could it be
that I was out of tune here in their home?

For when I, a stranger bird, joined their hymn
to heaven that had cleansed our common wood,

it was then, and only then, I understood.

Gulls

Sea gulls are not gullible.
They dive-bomb rocks with clams
and crash-land on the waves
to scoop up fish.

              I wish
I knew how far out to sea
they went, trailing ships,
floating in a slip-stream
of air.

      And what despair
of sea made them go
with Brigham Young to share
his Utah haven?

      Gullet-oriented,
yes, but sea gulls
are not
gullible.

Cormorants

Cormorants can fly
under the water like fish
risk fish's fate in nets.

Tracking Birds in Snow

A winter visitor has come my way,
inscribed a passage for me in the snow
that I could follow readily I know,
if I were so inclined today.

Too small for dove, perhaps a chickadee
has made these tracks and barely marked the crust
of frozen white. That tiny feet should trust
the numbing ice, amazes me.

Birds look so fragile walking on the ground.
Afoot, they're earth-bound prey to snowy owl
or sly, freebooting tabby on the prowl,
where furry menaces abound.

These twig-like footsteps cross a field, then go
toward the creek, an easy path to follow,
but in the trees that lie beyond the hollow,
I will lose sight of them, I know.

Kamikaze Osprey

The osprey circled, Kamikaze-like
it dived from the sky, defying death,
folding neatly into an arrow
before impact with the solid water.

It surfaced, gripping a fish in its claw,
shaking water from its dripping feathers.
It took two tries for takeoff because the fish
was big. The derring-do recalled a sailor

in '42 who scrambled over bodies
on the deck of the stricken *Hornet,* fire
and death the Kamikaze pilot's gift,
given with his own, young Samurai life.

"The violence of war was terrible,"
the sailor said. "At least it won us peace."
The osprey's phoenix-like return from death
won wild applause from those who watched from shore.

Honking geese flying
southward by night

Escape

set my soul sighing
in envy of flight.

Kitty Hawk, N.C.

Except for the wheeling gulls,
flight is animation suspended
    here at Kill Devil Hill.

The model of man's triumph
    extended on wire and block in
    emulation of how it
    must have been.

Fantastic, we think, that frail
    craft rising out of the dunes
    and
Wilbur running fast behind
    to catch his brother, should it
    fall,
Canvas, wood, bicycle sprockets,
    all in a heap in the sand
    and ruin.

But they were bird-men.
It has to fly! And it did; four
    times that first day.
Man at play on fairy wings.
Icarus must have known the
    same joy—being airborne.

Wilbur didn't see the Jennies,
    even.
But Orville knew the P-38s and
    more.
The score, by then, was frightening.
Did he wonder at the Luftwaffe's
    Guernica?
And who dared to tell him of Hiroshima?
Man's wings took him to the sun.
The plus, of course, is continents
    spanned, and man in space,

and a race, an incredible race
for Mars.
Soon man will soar faster than
light; then where will he be?
Day into night—out of time!

Somewhere, something was lost
and man is worse for its
dying.
One brave day there were men
who extended their wings
to soar with the gulls
for no more than the joy
of flying.

Man-Bird

Man is the unseemliest bird of all.
Envious since Icarus, featherless creature,
donned all manner of wax and wire
to simulate feathered flight.
With airborne mobility, he lost sight
of what it really was to be a bird
and kept his eyes fixed on the stars
forgetting current-wafted soaring joy.
The man in him overruled the boy.
Sail-planers, alone among birdmen,
find silence between the cloud and sod
to listen for the voice of God.

Paper Kites

There's something in all kids that loves a kite,
waiting for that March day to mark the spring.
The winter winds are still a-bluster now,
one last machismo blow, then zephyrs sing.

And I, some 60 springs, will join the kids,
enticing fragile kites to rise and sail.
Release from earth is never sweeter than
with tug of paper kite and long rag tail.

My children long since had their fill of kites
and humor their old mom with clucking sounds.
But I must do my flying while I can,
though part of me stays rooted to the ground.

If I were game enough on judgment day,
I'd give a fiver just to send my soul
up to heaven, spread-eagled on a kite.
Umbilicus can stretch beyond the world.

The Presence of Flying Fish

Journal entry, 14 June 1944,
on board the U.S. troopship *S.S. Matsonia*
0500 hours, 14th parallel south
the blue Pacific Ocean:

I've had today's one allotted shower
but this is a ridiculous situation, I can't
get rid of it, a sticky salt film
that won't wash off. My green K.P. dress
is equatorial-limp and salty-sticky, too.
We trust the good white ghost of the *Matsonia*,

plunging down-under through rolling green troughs
of salty-sticky stuff, her sleek metal
lines criss-crossed with camouflage.
Always riding her bow, never-ending
fresh legions of small flying fish
swim shotgun for us. They are our allies

leading us somewhere in a crazy-quilt pattern
like a sidewinder, that zig-zags our way into
the heart of a shooting war. The Southern Cross
is overhead and I am due on deck
to douse tin canteens in tubs of boiling
water. In half-light of shadows, I detour

to the rail to check on my little flying friends.
They're still there, exploding themselves forward
in phosphorescent arcs of silver. I know
I've learned to depend upon the shining presence
of small flying fish! The *Matsonia* and my
friends go faster than the enemy subs.

Journal entry, 2 February 1988:
This is just to note that I got there
and back all those many years ago.
My sterling little flying fish have never
left me. They are still taking me safely,
somewhere through angry, enemy oceans of
salty-sticky stuff that doesn't wash off.

I'm always humbled in the presence of flying fish.

51

V.

Love

"O lyric love, half angel and half bird,
And all a wonder and a wild desire."
—Robert Browning,
"The Ring and the Book," I

Swan Dive

Lithe, lissome, agile, strong-limbed
Daughter of my loins, seen arms out-
Reaching, time-arrested, sculpture in the air
At the top of your dive, I have to think
This split moment is mine.

All the coiled perfection of your body is
Unleashed and frozen at that point, youth
An eternity of torso, limbs, sinew, will,
Ascending. In those strong legs I still
Am young.

The rest of the dive is yours. Swift entry,
Water breaking in circles that will enclose
Your life, surfacing on other shores
In easy strokes; I cannot call the waters
Back—

Nor want to, content with the photo etched deep
In the red-veined recesses of my skull.
Your underpinnings are sound, grace inherited
Makes them responsive to flight. In part
My bequest.

Wrens

When
will we see
again
a bird
as small
and shy
as thee?

She-wrens
and he-wrens
together make
wee wrens
weighing only
milligrams.

City Sparrows

Flighty, friendly, chirrupy sparrows,
cat-conscious and quick as arrows,
fly in flocks
and alight by the dozens
to chatter and quarrel
with country cousins.

Giselle—Act II

Stiff-kneed, poking
in muddy rills and crevices
of a ploughed field,
a corps-de-ballet,
in classic white tutu,
follows Albrecht, the hero prince.

Albrecht, garbed in Levis,
dances among the Wilis,
dodging them, riding
a Ford tractor,
leaving in his wake,
worms, up-turned.

The Wilis, feet splayed,
waltz in the mist of encroaching moonlight,
plumes billowing in the wind.
Is there madness in the quickening
pace of their tightening circle,
the magic of their special spheres?

Where is Giselle?
Will she come, finally,
to save Albrecht from the Wilis?
Egrets are too beautiful to grub
for worms, or am I too taken
by appearances? Egrets must eat, too!

Pas De Deux
5 x 5 x 5

Belted kingfishers,
"his" and "her"—heated
aerodynamic
after-burners lit,
skim and flit in skilled

water-top duet.
Balletomanes prize
such poetic flight
that raises courtship
to heavenly heights

for earth-bound dancers
and free-flying birds.
Both earn curtain calls,
taking us aloft
for just a moment

where motion suspends
in air and flight ends,
hovering on death—
our fancy, of course.
Birds and dancers live

to fly again. I
will make a magic
lantern show of flight
and believe in it
indubitably.

Piping Plover Nesting Season

"The Fish and Wildlife Service, operators
of the Chincoteague National Wildlife
Refuge, will close the south end of the
beach, about 3.5 miles, to all humans
during the piping plover nesting season,
March 15 to August 31. Similar areas in
other refuges closed during nesting season
produce an average of 2 birds per nesting
pair. The area to be closed at Chincoteague
produces 0.19 birds per nesting pair."
(newsletter—Northern Neck of
Virginia, Audubon Society)

Oh, blighted, blighted Chincoteague
whose nesting pairs of piping plovers
produce but faulty chicks. Look over
the Northern Neck nesting stats—

stats can't get much worse than that,
0.19 birds per nesting pair!
Now that's a nest that's nearly bare.
Chicks are born but one-fifth there

to those poor piping plover parents.
Cursed by the Chincoteague connection
these chicks are less than chic perfection,
less than natural selection.

Here a tiny beak, a wing,
perhaps a foot, but everything
points to an 0.19 freak,
a partial plover, poor and weak.

—as Will, himself, would have said:

Sans teeth, sans eyes, sans voice to sing,
poor chick—sans nearly everything.

Red-Breasted Merganser Ducks

for all the glory of mating plumage,
live in fishy circumstances,
up-end and dive for finny morsels,
wooing their mates with water dances.

Were I a female duck, I'd be
most impressed to know a male
who could flap and run on water
and do a dance upon his tail.

Since I am but humble mortal,
I can't water-walk that way.
I'll be content to watch from shore
mergansers dance *pas de bourrée.*

> (*Pas de bourrée*: Progression on the points
> by a sequence of very small, even steps;
> one of the most beautiful effects in ballet,
> suggestive of gliding. *The Dying Swan* is
> largely composed of the *pas de bourrée.*
> —from *Ballet* by Arnold Haskell.
> a *bourrée* is also an Auvergnian dance,
> from Cassell's French dictionary.)

Hot Air Balloons

This is a birthday gift, of sorts,
for my sister.

Only an observant, old-bag of a sister would ever
fault you for getting in over your head
in a lot of hot air.

I know how much you love
the idea of hot air ballooning.
You know how much I
question the whole concept of the sport,
if it is a sport.

It doesn't start to match the hands-on
concept of real feathered flight with bald eagles,
soaring gulls, even those other fliers,
paper kites and flying fish.

That's flight I can get a handle on.

So—since you persist in looking
in your dotage for a
fountain-of-youth under a bag
of hissing, hot air, here's a birthday gift
with my love.

Enclosed, is a big, silk hot air balloon
that I've packaged and towed
back from the east coast, over
the prevailing winds, the jet stream,
all those mountains
and other misunderstandings
between us. You'll find it
right beside your cool green-white
backyard southern California
swimming pool.

Add your own racing colors,
as this is only a pretend
hot air balloon, anyway.

Since I do believe in flight and sisters,
if not in hot air balloons,
this birthday gift could be good for
one short hop in one of those bags!
The real thing. Send me a bill.

Just stay out of all that pollution
that hangs over Los Angeles.

VI.

Death

"Afraid? Of whom am I afraid?
Not Death, for who is He?
The porter of my father's house
As much abasheth me."
— Emily Dickinson,
"Time and Eternity"

The Leaf That Moved

Today the world turned round,
     the moon eclipsed,
stars swirled in the sky
     all because
one autumn leaf moved
     under my hand
when I brushed it from my thigh.

A small leaf, as fall leaves go,
     it fluttered up,
instead of down, then whirled
     a whorl of dance
in grand design tan-brown,
     twirled a perfect
pirouette and fell

back down among the leaves.
     On the ground I found
my velvet dancer, dead;
     a moth that whirled
with the world at night, steered
     by stars, mirrored
the sickle moon in flight.

The Origami Cure

"The flying crane brings happiness,"
she said, pulling the folded tail
which caused the head to move, the wings
to wave, but I could barely see

my mother or the paper bird.
A wet wash cloth was on my head,
sending trickles of water down
my back, wetting my cotton dress.

Too tired to move, my legs too short
to touch the floor, I sat upon
a bathroom stool, while mother talked
about wearing hats and heat stroke.

Then I saw my Sunday-schooled soul
soar out of sight, up to angels
and stopped just short of heaven's gate
by a white bird that beckoned me.

Through the wet kiss of cold compress,
I watched the flying paper crane
swoop down to bring me happiness
with mother's magic medicine.

Last Flight

for pilot, author, hero
Antoine de Saint-Exupéry,
when he was a little boy.

Perhaps it was a kind fate
that took Saint-Ex.
on that last flight,
from Bastia to Grenoble
in 1944.
He would be *démodé* today.
The now-hero hasn't time
—or inclination—
for finding little princes
or rescuing priests.

Honed in engineering schools,
polished in propaganda mills,
he emerges full-blown
as a hero-image.
We've always known
it could happen;
someday the machine
would swallow the man.

Just as Spain was
history's last war
where man fought man
for an idea,
even so was the curtain
ringing down on
the last of the Saint-Ex's.

True heroes aren't made,
they are born;
we've been making them
for some time now.
Perhaps we can program
the computer
to include a concept
of little princes.

I Sent My Song Aloft

I sent my song aloft, to play
upon the wind among the stars,
to sing the coolest summer song,
bring lyric warmth to winter hours.

I know its beauty is a thing
of fragile, woven words. They fling
bold metaphors into the path
of heaven's most poetic wrath.

That my frail song and I should part
on such good terms, so trustingly,
is all a matter of the heart,
where wings and things that fly go free.

Dorie, Bandit, and Dollie Carpenter Youkeles

About the Poet

A Flight Odyssey, composed of the light and serious verse of poet **Dollie Carpenter Youkeles**, reflects her love of all creatures. She talks to all of the visiting and resident birds and animals at her Gloucester, Virginia, home. "A pair of great blue herons visits my dock on the Ware River every day," she relates. "I've named the large male 'Big Foot' for the tracks he leaves in the mud when he fishes for minnows. His smaller shy mate I call 'Jane, Jane tall as a Crane' for the character in Edith Sitwell's 'Aubade.'"

Youkeles' life has been an odyssey, much like the migration of birds, from the cold Alaskan winds to the warm tides of the Chesapeake Bay. Born of gold-seeking pioneer parents in Juneau, Alaska, she was raised in Seattle, Washington, and earned a Bachelor of Arts in Journalism/English/Literature at the University of Washington. She served as a WAC with the U.S. Army in the south Pacific during World War II. After the war, she took graduate courses in literature and poetry at Columbia University, New York University, and the New School for Social Research in New York and wrote for magazines. With her husband, an education advisor with the U.S. Army in France, she lived fifteen years in France and studied French language, civilization, and poetry at the University of Grenoble and at the Centre Mediterréan à Nice. Upon returning to the United States, they settled in Virginia. Their children, Lila and Peter, were born in Europe. Her last writing position before retirement was director of public relations at Virginia State University.

"I imagine writing music in the words of my poems," says Youkeles, "trying to embellish melody with rhythmic turns of phrase to surprise and please a reader." She manipulates the tempo of her lines, always aware of the weight of words and silences, because—she insists—"music and rhythm are important to me in writing my poetry," directly influenced by Ezra Pound, who suggested a system of giving weight to letters, sounds, and silences in his 1934 "The ABC of Reading."

Youkeles favors metered verse and thinks of herself primarily as a traditionalist. But she does write free verse as well, when—as she puts it—"the poem wants to go in that direction. ...You have to let it find its own cadences. I sometimes map out a poem in prose and let it marinate for a while and come back to it when it wants to be a poem."

Believing that obscurity is the *bête noire* of poetry, she maintains a plain-word vocabulary. And when she discovers the best cadence for a poem, it becomes magically harmonious, like chamber music. At her home on the Ware River, an estuary of the Chesapeake Bay, she cherishes the wealth of wildlife that greets her every day. Her plain-word, harmonious poems of the wonder of birds and all flying things wrote themselves into a sensitive and appealing collection.